HOW TO SPICE UP YOUR SEX LIFE

Bedroom Satisfaction Tips

STACY WILLIAMS

© Copyright 2019 by Stacy Williams. All rights reserved.

This eBook is reproduced below with the goal of providing information that is as accurate and as reliable as possible. Regardless, purchasing this eBook can be seen as consent to the fact that both the publisher and the author of this book are in no way experts on the topics discussed within, and that any recommendations or suggestions made herein are for entertainment purposes only. Professionals should be consulted as needed before undertaking any of the action endorsed herein.

This declaration is deemed fair and valid by both the American Bar Association and the Committee of Publishers Association and is legally binding throughout the United States.

Furthermore, the transmission, duplication or reproduction of any of the following work, including precise information, will be considered an illegal act, irrespective whether it is done electronically or in print. The legality extends to creating a secondary or tertiary copy of the work or a recorded copy and is only allowed with express written consent of the Publisher. All additional rights are reserved.

The information in the following pages is broadly considered to be a truthful and accurate account of facts, and as such any inattention, use or misuse of the information in question by the reader will render any resulting actions solely under their purview. There are no scenarios in which the publisher or the original author of this work can be in any fashion deemed liable for any hardship or damages that may befall them after undertaking information described herein.

Additionally, the information found on the following pages is intended for informational purposes only and should thus be considered, universal. As befitting its nature, the information presented is without assurance regarding its continued validity or interim quality. Trademarks that mentioned are done without written consent and can in no way be considered an endorsement from the trademark holder.

ISBN: 9781076927835

Table Of Contents

Introduction 7

Chapter 1: Satisfaction Basics 9

    12 Ways to Fully Satisfy Your Partner 11

Chapter 2: Set Up A Sexy Date Night 15

    Date Night 16

    Rules for Date Night 20

Chapter 3: Wow Your Partner With Romantic Gestures .. 23

    Be Romantic 23

Chapter 4: Learn To Be Seductive 29

    Be Sexy 29

    Seduction Tips for Men 31

    Seduction Tips for Women 34

Chapter 5: Be Spontaneous 40

    Keep It Spicy 40

Chapter 6: Learn To Experiment 43
  New Things 43
Chapter 7: The Benefits Of A Great Sex Life To Your Marriage 46
  Some Final Thoughts 46
  Wrapping Up 49

Introduction

At some point in life most adults would want to consider the possibility of marriage. Not to be taken lightly, there are a lot of corresponding elements that are usually weighted in before the ultimate step of marriage is taken.

As soon as you got married, it was like a curse came over your relationship. All of a sudden, that spark that was always there is now gone and there is no passion in the bedroom.

You think of your partner as more of a friend now. What happened that made things so bad? If you are living in a sexless marriage, then you need some help.

You are desperate to get that spark back in the bedroom. You want you and your spouse to feel that sexual tension and that desire for one another again.

Ever since you got married, things just haven't been the same and it is time that you did something about it. You have to jumpstart your sex life again and make it exciting. You have to get that passion back between the sheets and start enjoying sex again.

You can spice up your sex life and you can start it today

When your sex life starts to suffer, your marriage suffers. It's as simple as that. It's never too late to rediscover the passion or turn things up a notch in your relationship.

Get all the info you need here.

Chapter 1:
Satisfaction Basics

Some people decide to live together first to see if they are able to adapt to each other's quirky ways, however this is not always accepted by the elders neither is it condoned or encouraged.

For whatever reason an individual decides to take on the journey of marriage, it should be done with caution and preparation to ensure a higher possibility of success.

Trying to contribute equally to the marriage arrangement or relationship is important as both parties should understand that there is a part for each person within the marriage platform that should be taken seriously and without reservation.

The equality factor will greatly help to determine the commitment levels each individual is willing to contribute to the relationship in order to make sure it has a fighting chance of survival.

There are many ways to ensure both parties stay participative in the marriage arrangement and this would include being able to share all things, communicating well, being understanding and sensitive to each other's feelings and needs and many other positive contributing elements that will benefit the strength of the relationship.

Sometimes when things don't go as well as intended, there may be a need to seek outside help to get things back on the positive track. This help may include seeing a counselor, a marriage therapist or any other notable person whose main function is to get the couple back into the mode where some positive progress can be made.

Sex is also another important part of a successful marriage, and couple should understand the need to ensure this part of the marriage get the adequate amount of attention it needs.

12 Ways to Fully Satisfy Your Partner

If you are looking to fully satisfy your partner and you really want to enjoy your time in the bedroom, here are a few tips that will supercharge your sex life and keep you partner focused on how great you are.

1. Your love making session should not be a race to orgasm. Do not rush yourself or your partner. A slow start with gradual increase will give you more sexual pleasure than rushed sex.

2. Keep in mind that arousal times are different and unique to your sex. A woman requires foreplay to get warmed up and aroused. Foreplay before intercourse will intensify your orgasm and make the whole sexual experience more satisfying for the both of you.

3. Become an expert in the arts of gentle touching, caressing and kissing, playing with her ears, lips, inner thighs, belly button, breasts and even the toes. Vary the pressure of your touch, firm and gentle, pause and resume; make your foreplay interesting.

4. Most women see sex as an expression of love, and if they don't feel nurtured, they may not get aroused or come to orgasm. Love her well and earn her trust.

5. Once a woman is aroused she will have the natural desire for penetration. There is no alternative for a hard and strong erection. If for any reason, you are not able to get hard erections, you could try some safe male enhancement pills.

6. Match your breathing rhythm with your partners. Breathing in tandem will greatly increase sexual satisfaction. This is also a great way of feeling completely connected to your partner. Moaning and shouting with pleasure could intensely

arouse your partner.

7. When a woman reaches orgasm, it can be so intense that she needs a few minutes to recover and comeback fully. Let her enjoy it in your arms and then be ready to give her second orgasm.

8. Your sex life is primarily dependent on your libidos. If your partner has a higher libido than you do, learn to compromise. Try some additional stimulation so that he can get into the act.

Explain to your partner that you need a lot of stimulation. Help him understand what you like better- a romantic evening, seduction or even some more foreplay. Having a frank discussion will help him understand your needs better.

9. If he has fewer libidos compared to you, try to get more active in bed. Get him aroused with what he likes best while at the same time making it clear that his feelings are of utmost importance to you.

10. You also need to change the roles you have in the bedroom at times. While we are often

influenced by traditional concepts in our bedroom, change is always good.

If you have been submissive in bed for a long time, get a bit aggressive for a change. If your role has been the dominant one, let your partner have a go occasionally while you just lie back and have fun.

This will give you a lot of variety and will bring the action right back to your bedroom!

11 Take your mind off intercourse for a few days. Instead, concentrate on erotic massages, feather strokes or just caressing. Excite your partner till she gets aroused and then back off. This will build the sexual tension and result in passionate lovemaking when you do decide to go for it!

Lastly add variety to your sex life. Try new sexual positions, play out your fantasies in bedroom, try aromatic massages, have sex in new locations like bathroom, Jacuzzi, swimming pools, gardens etc. to make it exciting. Try following these easy to follow tips and see how exciting your sex life will be.

Chapter 2:
Set Up A Sexy Date Night

For most people today, the idea of setting up a date night can be viewed as quite exciting and interesting. However, sadly most married couples don't understand the importance and significance, of this practice, as being part of keeping the marriage fresh and exciting.

It should be explored as an activity that would further enhance the marriage and create a lasting relationship that is both healthy and successful.

While the idea of date night works in theory, it often falls short because of expectations. This chapter will hopefully help define and give a fresh perspective on date night. I also hope to be able to provide some guidelines to help make the most of this tool.

Date Night

The following are some of the interesting ways individuals can go about creating sexy date nights to indulge in for the sake of keeping the excitement in their marriage:

Some find it rather exciting and sexy to take time off to indulge in a short get-away. This could come in the rather inexpensive form of the nearest local B&B.

This will allow the couple to get away from all the distraction that would usually take both their time in attention and instead allow them the leeway to focus on just each other.

Camping or simply dining under the stars is another inexpensive, yet exciting way to get the sexy romance going again, as has often proved to be the ideal sexy date night indulgence.

This activity also allows the couple for refocus on each other and leave all else behind for at least a little while.

Another great way to create a sexy date night would be to pick a favorite bottle of wine and some desert which is noted for its sexy appeal and then share a quiet night together enjoying these items while exploring each other's mind and body.

Wine and dessert when carefully selected have often proved to be the ideal ingredients that put people in the mood for a relaxing and enjoyable experience thus creating the ideal mindset to the sexy date night indulgence.

Many couples who have been together for a long time can fall into a routine. Often new things become a thing of the past, and as a result, intimacy starts to fade.

I'd like to start on what a date night looks like. Please keep in mind that everyone will have to adjust to their own needs and wants. That said, date night will look very different for the couple that has been married for 40 years and are in their 60's, versus the couple who has been married 5 years and are in their 20's.

Date night should have the look and feel of both comfort and connection. It should not be forced. If either party is not routinely excited about date night, there are issues on a deeper level and counseling may be a good first step.

Can you remember when you first started dating your spouse? It doesn't matter if it were 5 or 50 years ago. The newness of dating would lead us to do just about anything to be able to spend time with our new love interest.

Remember talking on the phone for hours, sending flowers and surprise visits? Or what about doing something that you had no interest in, but you did it anyway just to be with your partner. Why did that stop?

So many of us have fallen into a routine. And once

we "got" our new partner, we slowly over the course of time stopped doing all the things that we did in the beginning. This is why date night is needed.

The want and need to get to know your partner should not stop. In fact, it should grow stronger. And while it is equally important to have your own identity, do we actively openly share with our spouse?

I have often heard couples say "I know what he/she is thinking, so I don't have to ask". That is exactly the thought process that will end you up in a counselors office. I often say to my clients that if you have the same belief system you had at 25 when you're 75, you have wasted life.

So, if you're having the same conversations at 25 when you're 75, the same holds true. We must evolve. Far too many people stop growing and wanting to experience new things just because they are engaged in a long-term relationship. It's a trap.

So now that I have spoken about why it is needed and how it works, here are a few suggestions to help you turn date night into a great night.

Rules for Date Night

1. Do not talk about the kids, bills or work. This time is for the two of you to connect. Remember all the useless things you used to talk about when first dating? Do that. Or even better. Talk about where you are now.

Ask open-ended questions. Take an active role in listening. You two chose each other. All the things that have happened over the course of the years surely have changed both of you. Have you talked about them? Have you shared your deepest thoughts? Or did you hold back out of fear? The point that I am making is, talk about the real you. Make it all about the two of you tonight.

2. Get out of your comfort zone. Relationship routine can be deadly. Be open to spontaneous

adventures. Nothing brings people together like new experiences.

My wife and I were once at the state fair. We saw they had helicopter rides, and we both knew we had to do it. Out of the comfort zone and bucket list. Check! What about you?

3 Give a little, get a little. If you have different ideas of fun, take turns each planning a date. Sure you may have to sit through something that may not excite you. But, how many times did you do that when you were first dating? To connect intimately, sometimes the best thing you can do is to simply give.

4. I can not state this enough. Please put the phone down. Nothing will kill date night faster than you taking a work call, checking a text or responding to an email. I know that sometimes this will be unavoidable, but make it the exception. If you do pull out your phone, take a picture because you're having fun.

5. Should you double date? That's entirely up to you. But again, date night is about building intimacy between you and your spouse. So yes to the double dating, but try to leave it to once a month.

6. How often should date night occur? Once a week is optimal. There is an old saying that states, "you should meditate 20 minutes every day. If you're too busy for 20 minutes, make it an hour." I use the same principle for date night. Surely you can find 30 minutes a week for your spouse. Even if it's just time for coffee and connection.

Chapter 3:
Wow Your Partner With Romantic Gestures

Making the effort to extend a romantic gesture is usually always well greeted by the receiving party, and when this is well accepted, the chances of both parties benefiting from the outcome of the romantic gesture is indeed quite fulfilling.

Be Romantic

The following are some very simple and comparatively cheap ways of creating a circumstance to extend romantic gestures with the intention of wooing the other party and keeling the relationship alive and fresh:

Creating a weekly schedule that includes one date night is very important. If doing this on a weekly format is not possible, then both parties should commit to a date night at least twice a month.

Once the commitment is made the date night should be taken seriously and not canceled frivolously. It would show the level of interest of both parties when the date night is kept according to schedule.

Highly underestimated in the romantic gesture of being serious about setting aside a quiet time just for the couple to be able to communicate effectively.

Creating a relaxing environment where the conversation can be done in a leisurely and non-threatening manner is very much an enjoyable activity to indulge in.

Couples who are able to communicate on a variety of topics that don't necessarily revolve around their daily routines are usually able to see each other as new and exciting individuals who are constantly evolving and confident.

This will help to keep the freshness element in the relationship as both parties become more aware and interested in extending other romantic gestures towards each other and the possibility of staleness is firmly kept at bay.

Giving each other a full body massage is also another romantic gesture worth indulging in. This is both inexpensive and does not necessarily demand the expertise of a masseur's knowledge. Being able to extend this to each other will allow both individuals to explore and relax and enjoy each other.

Small, romantic gestures can be more powerful than their expensive counterparts. A way to a woman's heart is through her feelings. She needs an emotional connection to make everything feel right. The little things that show you consider her happiness and well-being make her feel appreciated, loved and adored. And that, my friend, is romance.

Is the concept still foggy? Here are a few ideas to try out:

Everyday Intimacies

1. Praise her regularly. Women love to give and receive compliments. It doesn't matter if you compliment the sparkle in their eyes when they laugh, or a new spice in the meatloaf. Just make it as specific and sincere as possible.

2. Touch her lovingly during everyday situations. Lay your hand on her lap under the dinner table or put your arm around her when watching television. Physical touch, without expectation, builds a connection and is the epitome of romance.

3. Call her by a pet name. Pet names are nicknames made perfect. A carefully given pet name sets your relationship apart from others. The right name shows you care enough to give her an intimate title

suited to your special bond. No matter how silly, the key is to use the name with confidence.

4. Bring her something without her asking. For example, when at the gas station, buy her favorite drink when you pay for the gas. Hand her the beverage with a kiss on the cheek. Or simply bring her a glass of ice water on a hot summer day. This is more about being thoughtful than reading her mind - simple and romantic.

5. Glance her way. Romantic body language goes a long way during the day to day activities. A special glance across the room while the kids are playing creates a special moment. Do it just right, and a deeply focused stare becomes an invitation for much more to come.

6. Show out like a teenager. Yes, you are all grown up, but teens know how to throw caution to the wind and enjoy life. Public displays of affection are très romantic. So, flirt, hold hands, kiss in public places and announce your love to the world.

7. Help out with "her" chores. Does she always load and unload the dishwasher. Take the initiative and complete this task for her. Better yet, when she gets up to clear the table, take the plates off her and say lovingly, "Honey, I'll take care of this. Go relax. You deserve a break." Don't ask. Just tell her you want to help, do it and do it how SHE likes it done. If she like the glasses on the top rack, put them there and don't forget to scrub the pots and wipe down the counter.

8. Pamper her properly. Offer to scrub her back when she is in the shower, and don't get in unless she gives an invitation. Give her a shoulder massage longer than 60 seconds. Go all out and paint her toes. Don't worry; the fellas never have to know.

Chapter 4:
Learn To Be Seductive

Being seductive come easy for some while for others, there may be a need to have some insight into the various methods that can be used to successfully take on the persona that will give the impression that the individual is indeed quite a seductress.

Be Sexy

Perhaps the most important element to understand about the art of seduction is being able to create the perception of allowing the other party to think their every whim and fancy is being addressed, and therefore indulged in.

Learning how to feel and extend this natural aura

or power will help the individual better understand the various ways of creating the ideal seduction methods that will help them keep any relationship exciting and alive.

One way of learning how to be a successful seductress would be to constantly study and understand the other party's mental and physical makeup.

Using self-discipline, will power, patience and coquetry are important in the quest to create the ideal seductress mode. Learning the art of the power of persuasion, influence, and enticement is important as this advantage will give the individual a better chance of coming off as a seductress than a needy individual.

Taking the trouble to be well groomed and indulging in the art of personifying the aura of sexiness is also advantageous and will help to promote the individual as a seductress.

However, it should be noted that there is a fine

line between presenting oneself as a cheap tart and as a refined yet sexy seductress and in being able to get a good understanding of the difference will allow the individual to exploit the benefits thoroughly.

Tools such as an enticing yet light perfume, simple and delicate looking jewelry and clothing that is complimenting to the individual's form would be a good starting point.

Seduction Tips for Men

Flirt a Little

What do women find seductive? First, for women, seduction starts in the mind, not the body. You wife needs to feel cherished and special. And they need some pampering and playfulness, a zone of relaxation. Flirting, in other words.

It's hard for her to switch from being a responsible adult, taking care of the chores and kids, to making love, unless she first switches her mindset.

Remember how you went about it in the early days of your relationship? I doubt very much that just reached over and grabbed your girlfriend when she was trying to fall asleep after a hard day. But a lot of you seem to be using this approach now. (So I've heard.)

Seduce Through Housework

Housework is directly linked to sex in the mind of a woman, and not in a good way. You probably know that your wife has some resentment over you not helping enough with the housework. Instead of getting into interminable discussions about what's "fair," look at it this way: A woman who feels like the maid does not feel like a sex kitten. What you prefer is up to you.

Also, a messy house is an anti-aphrodisiac for a woman. That's why she loves to go away for romantic weekends. Relaxing in a beautiful room she didn't (and won't!) have to clean-now that's seductive!

Warning to men: a man's response to this information is often to do one task and expect instant gratification. If your wife has years of resentment over housework, do not clean the kitchen once, get rejected and say: "It doesn't work!"

Take Love Lessons

Once you are in bed, do you know what to do? I'm not trying to be harsh, but I'm sorry, the plain truth is that a lot of you don't. This is not completely your fault.

A lot of times in the early stages of a relationship, women care more about romance than sex and are less demanding. So you don't need to be as skilled. And newness itself makes sex fun and exciting.

But sex with you is not new anymore. Your wife has a mortgage and kids, and maybe more concerns about her health and body image. You have a lot more competition for her attention. You've got to really know what pleases her to keep her interested.

Or, maybe she never really spoke up about what she wanted. Maybe you never got into the habit of talking to each other about what you like. This is why a lot of couples are out of sync in bed. And it can be hard to start that conversation if it's been off the table for years.

You don't have to make a big deal out of it. In fact, it's probably better not to. That can create pressure. Just a gentle question here or there, and you can get to know each other all over again.

The next time you wish for more spice in your bedroom, don't think: "What's wrong with her?" Instead think: "Am I being seductive?" That's when things will start to change.

Seduction Tips for Women

Seducing men can be a game to some but it does

take some time and effort to be totally good at it. Like a talent or gift, it should be honed and developed for you to start seducing men as easily as breathing.

Every woman can be an expert when it comes to how to seduce men --- first of all, you should try to have the right attitude and the mindset to do it. So without further ado, below are the top nine techniques on the art of seducing men --- made especially for you:

Be a little sexier than usual.

Well, that's if you're not dressing up sexily all the time of course. Being sexy is more than showing some skin and it takes a certain amount of attitude to be more than just a pretty face. Feel sexy inside and out and you'll be glowing with an undeniable aura of seduction and appeal.

Make eye contact.

The eyes never lie and nothing can beat it more

when you know how to keep and maintain eye contact with a man --- it means you have confidence and you know how to carry yourself around guys. The eyes can tell everything without the use of words and you can always shyly glance away if you want to --- teasing his mind and imagination to no end.

Leave something for his imagination.

Never be too easy to get, it kills the thrill. Men would like a little challenge and you should learn to play a little hard to get. It makes your flirting and seduction journey far from dull and boring. Well sure, women love to talk but try to hold up some information so he'd come back for more. Mystery and intrigue can work for men too!

Get close.

Getting close and leaning over is a sign of intimacy. Do you want to seduce him big time? Initiate the first move without appearing too desperate for attention. Guys have a thing for charming lovable women so go ahead and play the part. Of course, we're not saying you go over there and pretend like someone else --- just try to be a little adventurous for a change.

Smell Great:

A survey showed that eighty-nine percent of men said that the scent of a woman made them that much more attractive. Pick out a fragrance that your guy really likes. Once he smells you, he'll be unable to resist you the rest of the evening.

Feel Sexy:

Confidence gives a major boost when seducing a man. Spend a day pampering yourself and making yourself feel even sexier than you did before. Go to the spa; get a bikini wax or your hair done. Whatever makes you feel sexy all over. This will help in seducing your man and make you all that much more desirable.

Surprise Him

You could do this in many ways. You could join him in the shower one morning when he isn't expecting you to. Offer to wash his hair and back for him. Just having your soapy hands on him, teasing him, will get him going.

You could also be very sneaky when surprising him. Take a picture of yourself with a digital camera. Wear something he just absolutely loves. Now crop out certain parts of your body and email or send them to his work periodically. Save the best ones for last and by the end of the day, he'll have the whole picture and be ready to come home!

Be playful and fun

There are many games for partners to play. You could choose a board game or even dice. There are two dice that you roll and one dice says what you have to do and the other says where you have to do it. This can be very fun and playful yet still seductive if played right.

Use your imagination

Think of different creative ways to seduce that you would never have thought imaginable. Be daring and different. This is a great way to seduce him because neither of you would expect you to do something like that. If you go out to eat, sneak off to the bathroom and remove your sexy panties. When you get back to the table, hand them to him under the table.

Chapter 5:

Be Spontaneous

It is rather unfortunate, but most people tend to eventually fall into a comfortable routine that usually leads to some level of staleness in a relationship.

Keep It Spicy

In most cases, the creeps in gradually and for the most part goes unnoticed until one party becomes distracted with unhealthy outside interest.

One way to ensuring the relationship does not become boring or stagnated; both parties should ensure there is some level of spontaneity constantly indulged in.

For most people, the main reason for eventually falling into this rut lies in the fact that they have become too comfortable and thus almost too lazy to make an effort to be spontaneous.

The following are some ways to explore in the effort to stay or create spontaneity within the relationship:

Listening is a very important tool that can help to create a spontaneous moment within the relationship. Often people fail to listen to each other and thus end up missing important bits of information that can be used to create or arrange exciting events or date scenarios.

Jumping at the chance to try new things will also help to keep the "spice" in the relationship as both parties will then be privy to constantly see and surprise each other with their mental and physical reactions. This will also give both parties and insight into each other's lives.

Other ways of being spontaneous would be to

create little surprises for each other.

This could take on various different forms such as, preparing a special favorite meal, or trying a new recipe that is thought to be something the other party would be delighted to indulge in, arranging for a night out, but doing an activity that would not normally be indulged in, arranging a surprise getaway for two, and any other activities that would be characterized as exciting yet new.

Chapter 6:
Learn To Experiment

It is often more difficult for women to experiment than for the man. Men are generally more adventurous and are able to handle surprises well and in some cases thrive on it. Therefore in order to keep the marriage hot and sassy, both parties should indulge in the occasional experimentation of a new thing or two.

New Things

The following are some tips on what areas to concentrate on when indulging in the experimentation phase of the exercise:

Be a siren – this is a sure fire way of getting the other party to sit up and take notice. Most women tend to neglect their general appearance and often give more common excuses such as no time, too much work, home pressures, children and any other mentally and physically consuming activities.

However, when one party takes serious measure to look sexy and alluring, the corresponding response is usually quite orgasmic as the shock alone of being presented with an individual who has obviously gone to so much trouble to be different present an excitement all of its own.

When it comes to the bedroom antics, researching new and exciting ways to have sex could also help to put the sizzle back into the tired condition of the sex life of a couple.

There are many books and websites that are designed to genuinely help individuals who seem to have gotten themselves into a rut when it comes to their sex life.

Trying new positions, talking sexy and even taking on a totally different persona when in the bedroom will help spice up things.

Most therapists would recommend a session of sensual massaging instead of actual full-on sex, and if the eventual outcome leads to a steamy sexual encounter then it should be enjoyed as such. However, there should be no pressure on either party to actually engage in sex, as the idea is to establish sensual touching and intimacy.

Chapter 7:

The Benefits Of A Great Sex Life To Your Marriage

There are several reasons as to why sex seems to play such a pivotal role within the marriage relationship and for those who are interested in maintaining the "spark" some serious thought should be given to exploring the benefits of great sex and its impact on the marriage arrangement.

Some Final Thoughts

The following are some of the benefits commonly given when a couple is able to enjoy a good sexual relationship within the marriage perimeter:

Sexual intercourse helps to burn calories. Though

most people may think of sex as a fun way to burn calories especially when the gym is more often the place where the calorie busters are usually associated with this need, sex is also known to be able to produce similar results and is a more natural way of getting and staying nimble and in shape.

Another benefit of a great sex life within the marriage is that it keeps the couple closer and more intimate thus creating an ideal and warm family unit that is both conducive and comfortable to all who are part of the family unit.

Great sex does teach each party to be giving and less selfish and this extends into other parts of the couple life too, where they are more willing to have the give and take attitude as opposed to always taking or expecting to be on the receiving end.

Besides this, it also helps the individual to have a more complete and healthy body and mind condition.

Having frequent sex is good for the heart and lowers the stress levels of anyone, thus the need to consider this as an ideal way to relieve stress.

Wrapping Up

Making your sex life interesting through the years of marriage can be a challenge. It has truly become a challenge that most women are faced with finding techniques, tips, new ideas and many other ways to spice up your sex life and to please your man in bed. Here are some of them that you might find useful.

Don't stick to the same old routine and change venues. It is a common knowledge that marriages and relationships can dwindle down or lose spark after a few years, so don't allow your relationship to follow the same path. Even in the bedroom, you have to find some ways to spice up your sex life and break that monotonous lovemaking routine.

You can explore other exciting places to do the lovemaking or you can explore other positions.

Indeed, it doesn't have to be always in the bedroom. Discover the many ways to please your man in bed as well.

It may be through what you eat. Some effective ways to spice up your sex life may be through what you eat. If you are the cook in the house, adding some of the healthy aphrodisiac foods can be one of the great ways to spice up your sex life. Oysters are one of the best and most popular aphrodisiacs that you may want to add in your diet.

Check what you are wearing to bed. If you are now wearing that oversized T-shirt instead of that sexy lingerie, you might want to start spicing up your sex life by being sexy in bed.

Keep in mind that men are easily turned on by what they see - so play with their eyes.

It's all in the mind. Great lovemaking is aided by the power of the mind. If your mind is not conditioned to enjoy lovemaking, the act can eventually become a chore. Keep in mind that intimacy and lovemaking are major elements of marriage and keeping them burning alive is a great challenge in the relationship.

You may want to condition your mind by practicing meditation or even learning to focus on the act, being aware of your body's sensations and really enjoying the act.

Pay attention to the non-sexual ways of pleasing each other. You may say this is for women, but most men would surely appreciate some gentle massage after work. Hugging your partner and taking time to touch each other's body without getting to that sexual zones can be a great way too to enhance your intimacy and strengthen your relationship too.

Yes, you can talk about it out of the bedroom. Putting the topic out of the bedroom can also be a good way to ignite the feelings and passion with one another.

Learn to flirt with each other. You can email him, talk to him on the phone, or some other creative ways to tell him how much you want him. Be careful with this tip though, especially if there are children around and when you are calling him on the office.

And yes, you can talk dirty. Talking dirty has now become one of the ways to spice up your sex life, as it turns on men too. However, you have to be careful and learn how to say things, what to say and the right place to say it to make you successful in seducing and spicing up your sex life. Be careful also of some things that you should never say too. There are definitely dirty talks that can also turn off the partner, so be aware of them.

These tips can be simple but they can also be a good start in keeping the passion alive between you and your partner.

In order to make this happen, try something completely different. Try giving them sensual kisses on the neck and ear and this will lead to something.

Typically, a passionate kiss is a good indication that you want to take things further. Passionately kiss and feel your partner's body next to you. This will make you want them and will be a great way to get that passion back in your bedroom.

Also, you can try introducing lubricants and edible treats that may help to spice things up as well. Some sexy chocolate sauce and whipped cream can really make things spicy.

Sex for better or worse has always been a focal point in most peoples' lives, thus being able to enjoy a great sex life within marriage is often the basis of a good and strong relationship.

Printed in Great Britain
by Amazon